NORTHUMBERLAND YESTERYEAR

An album of photographs of life in Northumberland between 1860 & 1930

Edited for the Northumberland Local History Society

by

ROBIN GARD

1978

ISBN 0 85983 107 8

Published by FRANK GRAHAM 6 Queen's Terrace, Newcastle upon Tyne NE2 2PL

Printed by Howe Brothers (Gateshead) Limited

ILLUSTRATIONS

THE NORTHUMBERLAND LOCAL HISTORY SOCIETY

The Society was founded in 1966 to draw together the many groups and individuals interested in the history of Northumberland. During the past twelve years it has helped in the formation of local history societies throughout the County and one of its main functions now is to keep the two thousand or so members of its twenty-nine affiliated societies in touch with each other. It does this through a central committee of all the societies which arranges each year a One Day School, a day Conference, and a Round the County meeting to enable its members to explore the County with greater knowledge, purpose and pleasure.

The Society is keen to make a permanent contribution to the recorded history of the County. It promotes projects in which the local societies can combine to record neglected aspects of the County's history, it publishes articles in its magazine *Tyne 'n' Tweed*, and it aims one day to fill in some of the territorial and subject gaps in the standard histories of Northumberland.

Applications for membership and for information should be sent to The Secretary, c/o Northumberland Record Office, Melton Park, North Gosforth, Newcastle upon Tyne, NE3 5QX.

INTRODUCTION

In 1970 we published our first book of photographs entitled *Northumberland at the Turn of the Century*. It covered the period from about 1890 to the beginning of the First World War. It sold out very quickly and copies found their way into the homes of exiled Northumbrians in many countries.

This, our second collection of photographs, covers a wider span and takes us into the 1930's. For some of us, many of the pictures will only be reminiscent and nostalgic, but for the majority they will provide an interesting and accurate look at a not very old but a very changed social scene.

In 1970 we were a fairly new Society. Today we are 'parent' to twenty-nine thriving local groups whose members not only enjoy studying Northumberland's long and fascinating history but are well aware of the need to record that history. The carefully taken photograph, accurately dated, is one way of doing just that.

In 1914 the camera was something on a tripod in a studio; today a veritable army of camera-carrying sight-seers traverses the countryside. Even children can 'take' history in pictures.

I wrote in our first publication:

> "when new things come, old things go" and
> "memories die with every generation"

Old things are still going - unphotographed. Memories are still dying - unrecorded.

I hope this book, like the first, will stimulate a greater urge to provide for those who come after us a picture of life today made by ordinary folk like us.

Ellen W. Mitchell

President

ACKNOWLEDGEMENTS

The new local awareness of the importance of old photographs as historical records, stimulated partly by *Northumberland at the Turn of the Century*, published in 1970, has encouraged the Society to prepare this second album. Many more photographs have come to light since the earlier book and the first thanks of the Society must go to all those members of the local history societies in the County who have collected photographs for the book and in many other ways have made its publication possible.

The Society particularly thanks its President, Mrs. E. W. Mitchell, O.B.E., for her Introduction, Mr. R.M. Gard for arranging and captioning the photographs, and Mr. P. R. B. Brooks, Mr. I. A. Buchanan, Dr. C. M. Fraser and Mr. G. Long for their work on the editorial sub-committee. It is especially gratifying to all members that Mr. Frank Graham, one of their own number, should have agreed to publish the book on behalf of the Society. Special thanks are also given to Mrs. W. J. Kennedy and Miss O. Douglas, and to Mr. J. Bolton, of the County Record Office staff, for essential secretarial and photographic work respectively.

Regrettably, it is impossible to acknowledge individually the kindness of the many societies, institutions and private persons who lent countless photographs from which the final selection was made, but the Society warmly thanks all concerned and, in particular, the following for permission to reproduce the published photographs:

L. Baxter: 83; Belford L. H. S.: 2, 81, 101, 102, 110; Bellingham & N. Tyne L. H. S.: 72; Bellingham P. C.: 22, 23, 98; C. Beveridge: 12; R. Boston: 74; P. R. B. Brooks: 6, 35, 58, 77, 97, 111; R. Browell: 8; Major A. S. C. Browne D. L.: 15; Mrs. B. G. Carmichael: 61; F. M. Cowe: 57; P. T. Deakin: 92; Mrs. P. Dower: 16; Mrs. J. Fagan: 96; Dr. C. M. Fraser: 34; Felton L. H. S.: 105; Mrs. J. Gleghorn: 42; Miss M. V. Howey: 70; Miss N. Humphreys: 79; W. R. Iley: 89; A. Jensen: 37-39, 44, 93; Mrs. M. Kerrison: 48; W. Lockey: 36; J. A. Macrae: 50; E. S. B. Martin: 21; S. B. Martin: 4, 10, 40, 95; Newcastle City Library: 24-27; 31, 32, 78, 80, 82, 84, 85, 87, 100; North of England Institute of Mining and Mechanical Engineers: 1; Northumberland Record Office: 13, 14, 20, 28-30, 33, 43, 52, 55, 59, 60, 62, 64. 68, 69, 86, 88, 94, 103, Others: 9, 49, 67, 99, Ponteland L. H. S.: 109; R. Aln & Breamish L. H. S.: 17, 63; J. Robinson: 53 71, 73, 75, 91,; Mrs. G. E. Robson: 5, 7; Rothbury L. H. S. : 90; Mr. Sims: 66, 106, 107; Miss D. Stokoe: 65; W. R. Sullivan: 51; A. Tynan: 45; Tyne Industrial Archaeology Group: 18 ,46, 47; Mrs. E. M. Urwin: 11; J. V. Waitt: 54, 56; Wm. Ward, photographer, Bedlington: 19, 41; C. R. Warn: 104, 108, J. Witherspoon: 76; T. Young: 3.

SCHOOL DAYS

1 The tally boy of New Hartley Colliery who identified most of the 204 bodies recovered after the tragic accident on 16 January 1862. Thirty six of those killed were boys.

2 The girls of Warenford School, founded in 1837 by the British Society which advocated undenominational education, with the schoolmaster, possibly Thomas Oliver, about 1890.

3   A reading lesson at Coxlodge School, Gosforth, interrupted for a class photograph, about 1912. There are some 50 children under the charge of the teacher, Miss Harrison, and although posed, their general attitude conveys an impression of firm discipline.

4   The Blackett family of Wylam established a school in the 1840's for the children of their employees at Wylam Colliery and a British school (on the right) was built in 1854. A new school in Falcon Terrace was opened in 1910, and this photograph of the pupils outside the master's house was taken shortly before the move.

5 In 1928 children appear to have travelled to the Hott School, Greystead, on horseback, by bicycle, and on foot. The teachers are Miss Dagg (on the right) and Miss Cousin (by the gate).

6 A relaxed group of happy children at Barrington Colliery New School, with Ben Birkely, the school master (1882-1923), and Vera Birkely, his daughter and assistant teacher, 1913. The school had opened the previous year.

7   Eva Boyes, maid at Charlton House, Tarset, pumping water, about 1905. Domestic service was almost the only work for girls leaving school at this time.

8   Carrying water, outside Trail's cottages, Painshawfield Road, Stocksfield, about 1910. Fetching water from streams, wells, stand pipes, or village pants was a daily drudge for country and colliery village families until the provision of mains water from the 1930's onwards.

DOMESTIC LIFE

9 Wash day was hard work for a pitman's wife in the days when water had to be carried, clothes washed by hand and often dried around the hearth, and the iron heated on the hob. However, the poss stick made the actual washing a little easier. Here, a housewife is seen with poss stick and tub in the back yard of her house in Seaton Delaval, about 1930.

10 Delivering milk to Phoenix Row, Bedlington Station, about 1910. A boy could earn a few pence a week helping the milkman on his daily rounds. The colliery houses in this row were built in the 1850's and had one room down, one room up, and a pantry. The pony in the photograph is reputed to have been 32 years old.

11 Isaac Huntington, farmer of Shaws Farm, near Hexham, then aged 81 years, reading his newspaper—a daily habit after delivering milk—while his wife Mary rolls out dough on a baking tray to make bread and scones, about 1920.

12 Ramsay MacDonald, then Prime Minister, with his daughter and his personal detective, being made to feel at home by Mr. and Mrs. N. Beveridge (both standing) in the kitchen of the Bridge of Aln Inn, 1931.

13 Tea party, Mitford, August 1908.

14 Canon R. C. MacLeod, vicar of Mitford
(1896-1934) at his writing table, 1893. The Canon
was a keen photographer with a talent for recording
natural scenes of people at work and leisure. Several
hundred glass slides of life in and around Mitford,
and other subjects, which he made to entertain
his family and parishioners, survive to provide an
important record of thirty years of village life.

15 Indoor staff of Alexander Browne of Doxford Hall, about 1899. Front row (from left): head laundry maid, footman, cook, Rose Davies the children's nanny, footman, head housemaid. Back row (from left): general duties servant, valet, nursery maid, scullery maid, housemaid, laundry maid, James Laing the under butler, and butler.

16 Thirty-one male members of the estate staff of Wallington Hall in Sir Charles Edward Trevelyan's time, about 1885. Eighteen of these are identified, including (back row, numbering from left): (3) Thornton, keeper, (7) Davison, sawmill, (8) Keith, gardener, (11) Hearn, butler, (16) Howie, gamekeeper; and (front row, from left): (3) Walter Hedley, park keeper, (5) Nixon, bailiff, (8) Tom Taylor, Bolt Cottage, (10) Tommy Bowie, woodman, and (11) Atkinson, coachman. Three masons, a joiner, woodman, rabbit catcher and two footmen are also identified.

SHOPPING

17 William Dixon & Son's store, Whittingham, 1896. Village stores at this time could supply practically all the household goods a family would need throughout the year. The staff and family are (left to right): J. Ewart, J. Johnston, E. Donkin, W. Donkin, W. Ross, Miss Ross, William Dixon, Lucy Layton, Mrs. Dixon, Henry and Will Dixon.

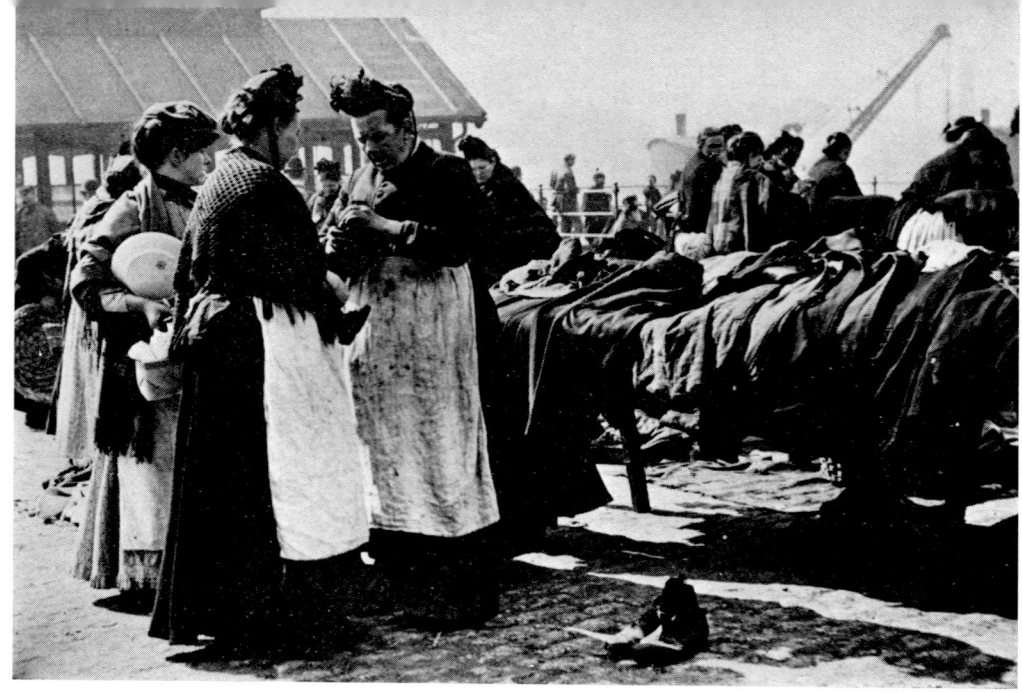

18 Clothes stall near the Seamen's shelter on New Quay, North Shields, about 1905.

19 Matthew Wintrip with his water cart outside the Rose and Crown, Bedlington, about 1910. He charged a penny a bucketful. It is not recorded whether the publican objected to this competition!

20 Shop assistants of the Bedlington Co-operative Society store posing to show the range of groceries available in the days when customers were given personal service, about 1905.

21 Thirty-nine members of family and staff of William Burgess and Sons, family butchers, outside The White Shop, their premises in Station Road, Ashington, about 1930.

22 Mary Ann Pigg in the doorway of her shop in Bellingham Market Place, about 1910. The carter's name was Maughan.

23 A complete set of horse harness made for the Ashington Coal Company and displayed by Frank Coulson, saddler and ironmonger, Front Street, Bellingham, about 1905.

24   Gosforth High Street, looking north from the junction of Hawthorn Road, with the County Hotel on the right, about 1905.

25   Morpeth Chantry of All Saints, founded before 1300, occupied by shops and by Young's mineral water factory, about 1910. St. George's Presbyterian Church (beyond) was built in 1860.

TOWNS

26   Alnwick Market Place, about 1910. Weekly markets were held on Saturdays for general produce and on Mondays for cattle. The Town Hall, built in 1736 with tower added in 1767, was used for all public and county meetings when Alnwick was unquestionably Northumberland's county town. Northumberland Hall (in shadow on left), a distinctive building with assembly rooms above and colonnaded shops below, was erected in 1826-30.

27   Waterloo Road, Blyth, looking west from Bridge Street, about 1905. The Theatre Royal was in Trotter Street (leading off in the right foreground) and beyond is the beginning of Turner Street. Ramsden's music shop and Hepworth the clothier's occupy the front of the old Central Hall, built in 1857. The tower and spire belong to the United Methodist church built in 1865 and the tall spire beyond is that of the English Presbyterian Church.

28   An everyday scene in Berwick High Street, looking south east towards the Town Hall with its classical portico, 150 feet high bell tower and spire and clock, about 1910.

High Street, Berwick-on-Tweed

29 Wooler High Street from the Market Place, about 1910. Few old photographs seem to exist which reflect the importance of Wooler as the centre of the social life and trade of Glendale. The Victorian fountain dominates the foregound of almost all views.

30 The Market Place of Hexham, like that of Morpeth, was also a thoroughfare but on Tuesday market days seventy years ago people crowding around the stalls in the open and under the colonnaded market itself, built in 1776, would have brought traffic to a halt. Cattle were also sold here until the Mart opened in 1888.

MARKET PLACE, HEXHAM

31 Bedlington Front Street looking towards the Market Place from the West End, about 1905. The first building on the left was then the Council offices and the third house, at one time the Brewery, was the home of Dr. Trotter. The Grapes Inn next to this was once the home of Bedlington's most famous son, Daniel Gooch, engineer to and later chairman of the Great Western Railway.

32 Morpeth Market Place, about 1890. The weekly cattle market once attracted cattle dealers, farmers, drovers, butchers, salesmen and street traders from the whole of the North East and was held in Newgate Street and Bridge Street, as well as in the Market Place itself, until 1905. The Town Hall on the left was rebuilt in 1870 but the facade of Vanburgh's 1714 building was copied. Beyond, the house and shops at this time continued in an unbroken line past the Clock Tower into Oldgate.

33 Haltwhistle Main Street about 1890. The narrow, winding main street of the town has defeated the efforts of most photographers to show Haltwhistle as the often very busy centre of the trade and social life of west Tynedale. This photograph taken from the Market Place looking west conveys instead an impression of the settled way of life in a country town in late Victorian England.

34 Saville Street, North Shields, in 1910 was hardly a street of great architectural pretentions, although several buildings are of character, but evidently the shops were quite busy on this sunny afternoon. The photograph is interesting also for the detail of several items of street funiture, notably the ornamental posts carrying the overhead cables for the trams and the ornate, solid lampstandards.

Saville Street, North Shields

COAL MINING

35 Two colliery officials, possibly in the Broomhill area, about 1930. The men are wearing blue kersey suits, breeches tied with tape at the knee, and leather skull caps, the typical outfit of underground officials. They carry yard length 'wands' and safety lamps.

36 Group of stonemen and sinkers employed at Sleekburn 'A' Pit to deepen the shaft to the Harvey seam, 1912. The man in a cranky flannel suit and leather helmet holding a trammel rod (used for measuring) is the chargeman sinker. The man in the front centre with the safety lamp is the deputy and William Lockey, who took the photograph, kneels at the left end of the front row.

37 Kirving out a nook in a narrow seam before blasting, about 1930. The hewer is working among loose stone removed from the top of the seam. The bottom caunch has been taken out to get the tub up to the coal face.

38 Hand drilling a coal face in a narrow seam cut by an arc wall cutter. The machine ran on rails laid on the bottom caunch which had been removed to a depth of two feet for the purpose, about 1930.

Miners like W. Lockey and A. Jensen who were keen photographers took scenes like these with simple pocket cameras, the light being provided by burning magnesium powder laid on the floor and lit through a torch powder by a match.

39 Filling a tub on a long wall face in a thick seam, about 1925. A candle is stuck in clay on a wooden prop next to the tub.

40 Callers-in, banksmen, tub tipplers, pick carriers and other pit lads, with the heap master and master's weighman, in the stockyard of Howard Pit, Netherton Colliery, 1910.

41 Doctor Pit, Bedlington, in the 1920's. The pit, sunk in 1854, had a steeple type engine house with a vertical engine. The boiler chimney is the one on the right, the chimney on the left serving as a flue for the underground furnace. The shaft and heapstead are in the centre and John Pit, sunk in 1908 as upcast for Doctor Pit, is on the extreme left.

42 Crank Row, West Moor Colliery, Killingworth, about 1910. From the left, Mrs. Wilson (in black) stands next to Mrs. Ferguson and baby, with Ethel and Alice Tudor just behind. The boy in the centre with one bare leg is Jack Ferguson. Few photographs showing colliery rows are known.

43 Old Benton Square, near Longbenton, about 1910. The cottages were built probably in the mid-19th century and would have had a single room downstairs, with ladder access to a space in the pantiled roof used for children's sleeping quarters. The lean-to pantries were added later.

44 Horse pulling coal bogies, Ashington, about 1920. The Ashington Coal Company laid a network of tram rails along the colliery rows to supply pitmen's coals and to remove the ashes.

45 Supplies being delivered, about 1925, to the remote Plashetts Colliery village in the North Tyne valley along the colliery tramway from Plashetts Junction on the Border Counties section of the North British Railway. Coal mining in the area commenced in the mid-19th century and finally ended in 1966.

THE SEA

46 "The Penny Ferry", a steam paddle ferry which carried passengers across the Tyne from South Shields to New Quay, North Shields, about 1910.

The usual dress of fishwives in North Shields, Cullercoats and elsewhere in Northumberland comprised a print bodice, coloured neckerchief, blue flannel skirt worn ankle length and having numerous tucks, a plain apron. home knitted stockings and strong shoes. The wicker baskets, carried strapped to the shoulder, were called creels.

47 (*below left*) Fishwives sorting herrings on North Shields Fish Quay, about 1910.

48 Elizabeth Taylor, otherwise 'Long Betty', a Cullercoats fisherwoman, about 1930. Thomas Storey, her husband, wrote a weekly column in the Sunday Sun.

49 The Tyne at North Shields, 1898. Two paddle tugs make towards the sea, passing the training ship "Wellesley" and another former naval vessel moored close to the north shore, details of which, including the High and Low Lights and the Fish Quay, may be seen. The 'Wellesley' was actually the former 74 gun 'Boscawen', reputedly the last commissioned wooden naval line of battle vessel, acquired by the Training Ship Committee in 1873. It was destroyed by fire in 1914.

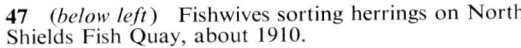

50 Loading whinstone in Craster harbour, about 1913. The harbour was built as a memorial to J. C. P. Craster, killed in the Tibet Expedition of 1904, and was completed in 1912. The Craster Whinstone Company of McLaren and Prowde Ltd. erected an aerial ropeway from the stone crushing plant in the nearby quarries to the stone store bin on the pier.

51 Sailing colliers loading at the Cowpen Colliery Company's staiths at North Blyth, before the staiths were set back to enable berths to be deepened and the channel widened in 1897.

52 Scotch fishergirls who worked their way down the East Coast, spending seven to ten days dealing with the main herring catch in each fishing port, are seen here gutting and barrelling the glut of herrings at Blyth for export to the Continent or London, about 1910.

53 The "Betsey Hughes" keel boat of Newbiggin by Sea, with its owner, R. Dawson, his family, crew and others on Newbiggin beach, 1904. These large herring fishing boats were crewed by ten to fifteen men. Straight sterned keel boats like this were made in Fife and known therefore as 'Fifies'.

54 Ploughing in the North Tyne valley, about 1920.

AGRICULTURE

55 Bondagers hoeing and thinning turnips at Kirknewton, about 1910. In former times the Northumberland hind or agricultural worker, as a condition of his yearly hiring agreement had to provide a woman worker, known as the bondager, to help at busy times of the year. The bondagers' customary dress was a broad brimmed straw bonnet over a scarf tied around the head and face to protect the complexion, a blue blouse and pink kerchief, a coarse woollen skirt and white apron, black stockings and hobnailed boots.

56 Gin-gan, North Tyne valley, about 1910. Horse powered machinery for thrashing corn and for other farm purposes was introduced in the late 18th century and, although superseded on large farms by steam powered engines, continued in use elsewhere into the present century, and the round or octagonal gin-gan buildings remain a feature of older farmsteads. The occasional use of this simple two horse gin-gan presumably did not justify a permanent buildnig.

57 The flitting, about 1880. The Northumberland hind was normally engaged for one year. Among his conditions of service were a free cottage, coals, grazing, hay or straw for a cow, corn for bread, and potatoes, as well as a yearly wage and money for the bondager supplied. Many hinds stayed with one farmer for years but many more moved from farm to farm, and the general exodus on 12 May was known as the 'flitting'.
The photograph shows at least four families, with all their possessions, resting outside the Lamb Inn, Ancroft.

58 Arthur Foster (on reaper) and lad mowing hay at Heddon Haughs, 1918. Most farm workers favoured corduroy trousers and waistcoats at this time. The high pointed horse collars were peculiar to Northumberland.

59 Field workers resting and enjoying their lunch bait in the harvest field, Mitford, about 1910.

60   Building a long stack, North Northumberland, about 1910. It was customary on large farms to build long haystacks measuring as much as 45 feet long by 15 feet wide at the base and rising to about 30 feet in height. The hay was raised by means of a simple apparatus comprising a pole, pulley, rope, jib and grab. The hay was brought on bogies to a central heap under the grab which was raised and lowered by rope and pulley by horse power. The completed stack would be trimmed and thatched.

61   Thrashing scene, about 1910. The introduction of the steam traction engine and mobile thrashing machine in the mid-19th century enabled the farmer to thrash his corn in the harvest field or in the stackyard at his own convenience. Photographs of thrashing in progress are rare, and the figures, unless posed, are usually blurred.

62 J. Brown's smithy, with thatched and slated cottages adjoining, which stood at the west end of Ponteland village, near the junction of the present Darras Road, about 1905.

63 Sheep clipping at Kidlandlee, about 1910. Kidland House (seen in the background) was built about this time by Captain Christopher Leyland of Haggerston Castle and stood 1250 feet above sea level. Only the stable block now stands.

LEISURE

64 Michael Bulmer and his wife Elizabeth making good use of the summer evening sun in the doorway of their cottage at Kit Shield, near Henshaw, about 1910. The cottage is now in ruins but would have had just one room, with a pantry and a cow byre adjoining. Although living in primitive conditions the agricultural worker and his family were often skilled and well educated. The photographer clearly sensed and has recorded the dignity of a well earned rest after a hard life.

65 Wrestling at the Chatton Sports, about 1910.

66 Serbian gipsies with performing bears and monkeys providing entertainment for a good crowd of spectators at Wooler, about 1905.

Servian Gipsys in Wooler

67 Allendale Show, about 1900. In country districts the agricultural show was the highlight of the yearly calendar. Prizes for horses, cattle, sheep and other livestock, for flowers and vegetables, for domestic skills, for deftness in farm work, and, not least, for prowess in running or wrestling, attracted numerous competitors and spectators who were entertained throughout the day by the local brass or silver bands.

68 Bothal Tenants' Annual Show in the field below the Castle, about 1900. The first Show was promoted by the Duke of Portland in 1880 to raise standards of stock keeping and husbandry among tenants on his Bothal Estate. As well as the usual livestock judging, prizes were awarded for such classes as the best managed farm, the best crop of turnips, the best garden and the best collie dog.

69 The photographer photographed! A brief stop on a cycle ride through
Warkworth to take a photograph of the village street and Castle, about 1910.

70 Hepple Morris Dancers organised by Miss Olive Buchanan Riddell practising in the grounds of Hepple
Whitefield, possibly in preparation for a competition in Newcastle, about 1913. Edith and Margaret Clark and
Harriet and Margaret Oliver are some of the dancers.

71 Potshare bowling was a miners' sport. The bowl was made of firebrick scrubbed out in a rough mould and covered with pitch and was made in various weights. The object was to bowl underarm over a measured distance in the fewest throws, or the longest distance in a set number of throws. Contests took place over the Newcastle Town Moor, Whitley and Newbiggin Links and other open spaces. The two bowlers in this photograph are Robert Armstrong holding a 25 oz. bowl and John Jefferson, about 1920.

72 A game of quoits on Wark on Tyne village green, about 1910. Quoits another predominantly miners' game, has ceased to be played.

73 Newbiggin beach, 1904. Although this was probably a Bank Holiday crowd, Newbiggin has always been a popular place for a day by the seaside. Newbiggin Church on the point was a welcome landmark for the local fishermen who on this occasion are using their cobles for pleasure trips.

74 Pierrots at Spittal, Tweedmouth, about 1920. The ground is now a putting green.

75 A tense moment for a good sized crowd watching Newbiggin Athletic F.C. playing an important game, on Newbiggin Moor, about 1911.

76 Jim Witherspoon being cheered to the winning post in Haltwhistle Market Place, having completed the 40½ mile Newcastle Exchange Walk of 1922 along the Military Road via Greenhead to Haltwhistle in 6 hours 49½ minutes, only 3 minutes outside the record time.

77 Allenheads in 1910. Although its days as the supply centre of a large lead mining community in the mid-19th century were by now a distant memory, the village still served a population of over 850 persons. It had three shops—that of William Pearson who also kept the Post Office is seen on the right—and John Shields, the proprietor of the Inn, operated a daily carrier service to Allendale.

VILLAGES

78 The Temperance Hotel, Stannington, about 1910. Until 1888 the village was part of the Morpeth estates of the Earl of Carlisle whose wife was a strong supporter of the temperance movement. She shared this interest with the Duchess of Portland whose influence is said to have deprived the fast growing town of Ashington on the Duke's Bothal Estate of licensed houses. The milk float at the gates seems appropriate. Two of the boys are in scouts' uniform.

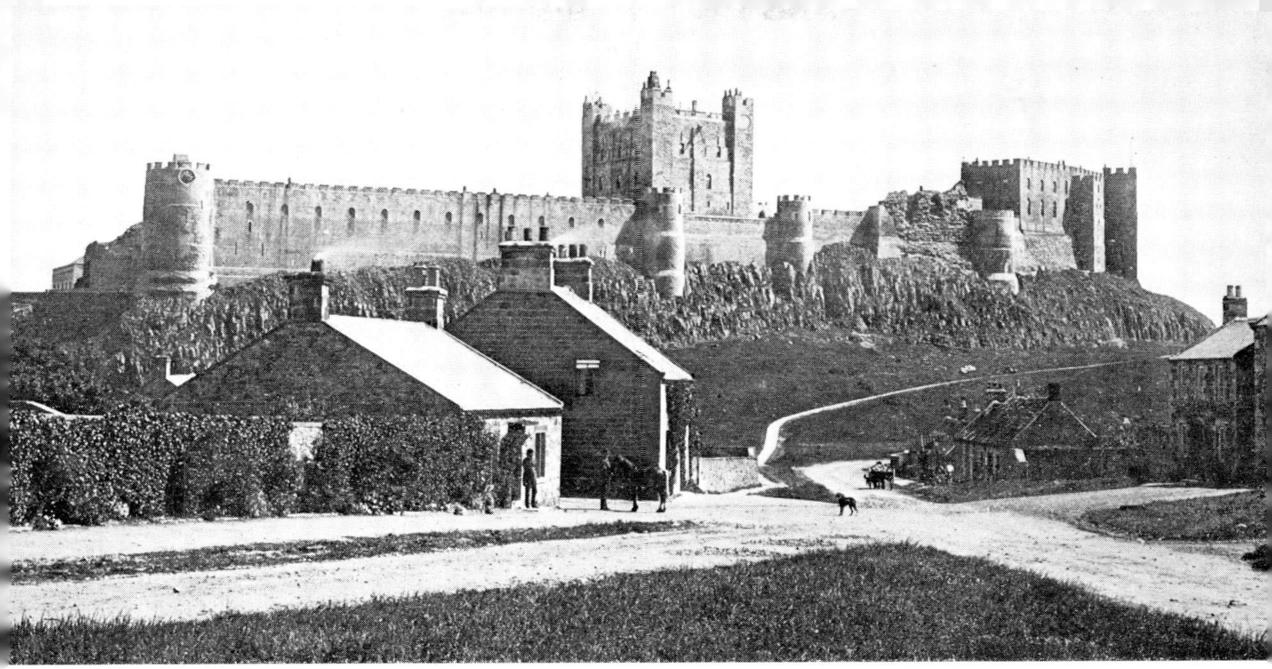

79 Bamburgh Castle seen from the village about 1905, shortly after its final restoration by Lord Armstrong who bought it from the Trustees of Lord Crewe. The keep, great hall and other buildings had been already restored in the 1770's by Archdeacon Thomas Sharp who was also responsible for the Crewe Trustees establishing a dispensary, a cheap shop, a woollen manufactory, day and boarding schools and other charities in the village.

80 Beadnell village street looking towards St. Ebba's church with its unusual tower and spire, and the Craster Arms on the left, about 1930. At this time about 15 families in the village depended on fishing for their living.

81 Belford main street could harldly have been quite as peaceful as this, even in 1900, for James Simpson, at the Blue Bell, advertised that commercial and cyclists business was a speciality and that his large hall seated 250 and offered good accommodation for picnic and other parties Luke Scott at the Salmon Inn catered for more regular custom. The building next to it with the coat of arms on the chimney was the County Court house.

82 Like many Northumberland villages before the First World War, Glanton in 1910 was practically self supporting. Its resident tradesmen and craftsmen included a builder, joiner, contractor, two ironmongers, blacksmith, two slaters, saddler, shopkeeper, draper, two grocers, baker, confectioner, two butchers, tailor, cycle agent, and a laundress. The Queen Head Hotel and James Scott's apartments provided for visitors and the Red Lion public house and Post Office catered for other social needs.

83 Alnmouth became a fashionable seaside resort in a quiet way in the mid-19th century and by 1910 its sands, links, golf club, boating, bathing and other amenities had also made it a popular place for a day by the sea. The Schooner Hotel, seen here on the left, and sixteen apartment houses elsewhere in the village, provided for holiday visitors.

84 Monkseaton in about 1905, when it was still a village before being enveloped by Whitley Bay. In 1891 its population was a mere 564 and even in 1901 it was still under 1,000, but by 1910 it had trebled in size. At this time William Hills was landlord to the Black Horse Inn, Mrs. Robinson had the Ship Inn (behind the tree), and Scott and Robson kept the grocers shop in Percy Terrace (in the centre).

85 A fisherman going home from the Harbour across Sanctuary Close towards Holy Island village, about 1910. The house next to the Priory ruins is the Manor House Hotel, and the footpath crossing the Close leads to the Crown and Anchor Inn and the Square.

86 Warkworth village street crowned by the Castle. This is almost exactly the view being photographed by the lady cyclist in number 69.

OCCASIONS

87 Horse procession, Morpeth, about 1905. A procession was a traditional feature of the customary twice yearly horse fairs held in the Spring and Autumn in most market towns. On such occasions normal business was suspended while all the town turned out to watch the event.

88 Pilgrimage of bishop, clergy and lay folk from the Roman Catholic diocese of Hexham and Newcastle to Holy Island on 11 August, 1887 to commemorate the 12th centenary of the death of St. Cuthbert, forming up to walk in procession to the ruins of Lindisfarne Priory.

89 Proclaiming Stagshaw Fair at the market cross, Corbridge, about 1910. In medieval times the fair, held on Stagshaw Bank on Whit Saturday and 4 July, had been one of the greatest in the North of England and even at this time it was still an important cattle fair.

90   The annual May Day procession at Rothbury, about 1910. James Johnson, for many years master of Thomlinson's school and town bandmaster, would doubtless have played a leading part in organising this procession.

91   Crowds assembing in Front Street, Newbiggin, for an August Bank Holiday parade of decorated floats and carriages through the town, 1910. Scarcely anyone can be seen not wearing a cap or hat of some description. Rutherfords, the chemist, and Maddison, the grocers (on the right), were two long established businesses.

92 Volunteers of the Northumberland Fusiliers marching out of Bondgate on their way to camp, 1907.

93 Peace tea, Woodhorn Road, Ashington, 1919. Only a few photographs of the numerous street parties which were held on such days as the official ending of the Great War and King George V's Jubilee in 1935 survive. As most of the children in the photograph were 13 years of age, many people alive in Ashington may recall the occasion. The photograph is labelled 1919 but the dress of some children and grown-ups suggests a later date.

94 Mary Marwood Nicholson, aged 16 years, the youngest employee of the Company presenting a bouquet to the Queen on the visit of King George V and Queen Mary to the North Shields docks of Smith's Dock Company, 16 June, 1917. The Queen made an exception and signed a photograph of the occasion.

95 The Prince of Wales, later Edward VIII, seeing pitmen's living conditions for himself, about 1924. The cottage is thought to have been in the Seaton Burn area.

RAILWAYS

96   British Rail locomotive 67241 pulling two coaches out of Lambley Station, 1948. The Haltwhistle to Alston
line was opened in 1852 and became the last branch railway in the County to be closed (in 1976). Its chief
engineering feature was the Lambley viaduct with nine arches of 66 feet span and seven of 20 ft. span, crossing
the South Tyne valley at 100 feet above the river.

97 'Puffing Billy', with driver J. Pratt and fireman J. Greener, at Wylam Colliery, about 1860. In 1862 Captain Blackett loaned the locomotive to the Patent Office Museum (now the Science Museum) in South Kensington. The Museum later purchased it for £200. The Colliery School, shown in photograph 4 is on the extreme left. This is almost certainly the earliest photograph in this collection.

98 The first train from Newcastle via Hexham at Riccarton Junction at the opening of The Border Counties Railway in 1862. The engine was made by E. B. Wilson of Leeds.

99 Seahouses station was the terminus of the four mile long North Sunderland Railway from Chathill on the main line. It opened in 1898 and was closed in 1951. The photograph shows the Company's first locomotive, 'Bamburgh', and two carriages which were built in 1883-4 and purchased in 1911-12 from the North Eastern Railway, about 1920.

100 A Newcastle bound train waits at Haltwhistle station on the Newcastle to Carlisle Railway, about 1910, while an engine prepares to join its carriages at the Alston branch platform on the right for the 13 mile journey across the bridge in the distance and up the South Tyne Valley.

101 Carriages waiting for passengers at Belford Station, about 1905. The elegant station buildings were designed by Benjamin Green and built in 1847-8.

102 Renewing a level crossing on the busy Newcastle to Edinburgh line, probably at Beal Station, about 1910.

ON THE ROAD

103 Shoppers and shopkeepers alike, and even a surprised horse, stop to admire some of the finest motor cars in the country parade through Alnwick probably during an RAC rally, about 1910.

104 Two Daimler charabancs owned by the United Company, waiting to start out from Ashington for London with football fans from the Collieries Welfare Sports Clubs, 1919.

105 The iron chassis, roughly sprung frame, solid tyres and padded seats of this chain driven Newcastle charabanc, possibly an Albion, promised a bumpy dusty ride ahead for this party photographed at Felton about 1910, but the ladies with their long coats and skirts, rugs, large hats and face veils seem well equipped and intent on enjoying the experience.

106 A steam traction engine owned by William Wilson of Preston pulling the trailers of an Austrian Circus which had been visiting Wooler ran out of control down the steep hill leading to the bridge and demolished the parapet, 1908. The damage cost only £29 to repair and the County Council sent the bill to Wilson.

107 Leyland motor wagon with which James Straughan and Sons operated their carrier serivce on the Wooler road, about 1920.

108 The Otterburn depot and garage of J. Foster with two service buses and three motor cars, 1923. The letters X and NL were the first two Northumberland registration letters and the car, NL7555, being filled from the Pratts petrol pump was owned by Mrs. Dickinson of Corbridge.

109 The photographer receives an RAC patrolman's salute, once every members privilege, as he records vehicles outside the garage of the Ponteland Motor Car Company, about 1925.

110 Road surfacing in progress on the A1 at Adderstone near the Bamburgh road junction about 1908. This narrow, winding section of the Great North Road has now been closed with the completion of the new Warenford Bypass in 1977. In 1908 the cost of repairing the A1 averaged out at £82 per mile.

111 Five ton Foden 4774 tipper, registration number X 4507, supplied new to the Northumberland County Council in September 1914. This vehicle was requisitioned by the War Department in the 1914–1918 War and ran for the War Department with fresh Wiltshire registration, AM 8742. Its last owner was Fred Robinson Ltd. of Stockton on Tees.